ABORTION

'Open Your Mouth for the Dumb'

GW00492846

ABORTION

'OPEN YOUR MOUTH FOR THE DUMB'

Peter Barnes

THE BANNER OF TRUTH TRUST

THE BANNER OF TRUTH TRUST
3 Murrayfield Road, Edinburgh EH12 6EL, UK
PO Box 621, Carlisle, PA 17013, USA

*

© The Banner of Truth Trust 2010
First published as *Open Your Mouth for the Dumb* 1984
Reprinted 1986
This revised edition 2010

ISBN: 978 1 84871 054 2

*

Typeset in 11/14 pt Adobe Garamond Pro at
The Banner of Truth Trust

Printed in the USA by
VersaPress, Inc.,
East Peoria, IL.

Contents

1. WHAT IS ABORTION ALL ABOUT?

In a comparison that is so apt that it has aroused widespread resentment, John Powell has referred to the widespread practice of abortion in our own day as 'the Silent Holocaust'.[1] The treatment of unborn children in the Western democracies can indeed be compared with the treatment of Jews in Nazi Germany. Most significantly, Dietrich Bonhoeffer, the Lutheran pastor whom Hitler sent to the scaffold in 1945, spoke as strongly against abortion as ever he did against Nazism. His views are worthy of quotation:

> Destruction of the embryo in the mother's womb is a violation of the right to live which God has bestowed upon this nascent life. To raise the question whether we are here concerned already with a human being or not is merely to confuse the issue. The simple fact is that God certainly intended to create a human being and that this nascent human being has been deliberately deprived of his life. And that is nothing but murder.'[2]

As early as 1933, as Nazi persecution of the Jews gathered

[1] Cf. J. Powell, *Abortion: the Silent Holocaust* (Texas: Argus, 1981).
[2] D. Bonhoeffer, *Ethics* (London: SCM, 1963), pp. 149-150.

momentum, Bonhoeffer saw clearly the duty of the Christian. He turned to the Word of God, and Proverbs 31:8 was often on his lips: 'Open your mouth for the dumb'.[3] This same duty rests upon the Christian in our own day as abortion has become widely practised and accepted.

An age of slogans and deadened moral sensibilities inevitably has many depressing features, but two of the more serious are the lack of clear thinking and the debasement of language. In many places, girls as young as eleven have had abortions and fourteen-year-olds have returned for their second operation. Yet they would not be allowed to buy liquor and usually would require parental consent before having their ears pierced (this consent is not usually required in abortion cases). There are government-sponsored campaigns against smoking by pregnant women on the grounds that the practice could harm the infant. And unborn children involved in automobile accidents have even secured compensation through the law courts. The government of New South Wales, Australia in 2004 introduced and finally passed legislation to protect unborn children against acts of violence—yet abortion was specifically excluded. Modern secular society increasingly suffers from a kind of arbitrary moral schizophrenia. In fact, there has been a subtle and pervasive assumption that pro-abortionists are sensitive, liberal and humane people who are articulate, intelligent, and in touch with the needs of modern living, while the pro-life side has been often portrayed as a group of dogmatic hard-liners who may even have leanings towards fascism. Vera Drake is canonised, and Gianna Jessen is an embarrassment.[4] One woman who had an illegal abortion

[3] E. Bethge, *Dietrich Bonhoeffer* (London: Collins, 1977), p. 207.
[4] Vera Drake was a British abortionist in the 1950s who was eulogised in a film of the same name in 2005; Gianna Jessen had the temerity to survive an abortion in 1977, and,

in the 1960s tried to claim that it was a case of 'Because I had sex, someone thought I deserved to die'[5]—such is the human propensity towards fantasy and self-justification.

In addition, the unborn child has been labelled a 'protoplasmic mass', 'just a clump of cells', 'contents of the uterus', or 'foetal tissue', while abortion itself has been called 'a method of post-conceptive fertility control' or, more simply but just as deceptively, 'the termination of pregnancy'. This demeaning of words has had profound effects; language is to be treasured, and it was not for nothing that Augustine of Hippo referred to words as 'precious cups of meaning'. In the present situation, however, words have been used to disguise reality rather than to reveal it. Therefore, before proceeding any further, we should be very clear as to what exactly takes place during an abortion.

There are five main methods that are used to end the life of an unborn child. Recently much publicity has been devoted to the so-called 'morning after pill'. Normally, there are two stages to the process, and these two stages are separated by about a week. At first, the anti-progesterone, RU486, is administered to the mother to induce the death of the unborn child. Because RU486 by itself has a high failure rate, a second drug—a prostaglandin—is administered a few days later to expel the foetus from the woman. The actual expulsion will usually take a few more days.

Secondly, for early pregnancies, there is the dilation and curettage technique. The cervix is first dilated, and a tube is inserted into the mother's uterus. This tube is attached to a suction apparatus which tears the little baby apart and deposits

with good reason and impeccable credentials, has campaigned against the practice.

[5] Cited in J. Hadley, *Abortion: Between Freedom and Necessity* (London: Virago Press, 1996), p. 68.

him or her in a jar. A curette is then used to scrape the wall of the uterus to remove any parts of the baby's body that might still be present. Often the suction tube is not used at all, and the curette is simply used to cut the baby's body to pieces and scrape out the placenta.

This technique is usually considered to become too dangerous for the mother after about the third month of pregnancy, so a saline abortion is employed. This third method might be called salt poisoning, but it has become far less common in the West than it used to be. The procedure is gory enough. A solution of concentrated salt is injected into the amniotic fluid in the sac around the growing baby. The salt is absorbed by the baby who is poisoned to death after about an hour. The outer layer of his skin is burned off by the salt, and about a day later the mother goes into labour and delivers a discoloured and shrivelled-up baby. A few such babies have been delivered alive, although they rarely survive long. Prostaglandins can also be used after the third month of pregnancy. Prostaglandin chemicals are injected into the uterus, causing the mother to go into premature labour and deliver a dead baby. However, prostaglandin babies have been born alive, much to the embarrassment of some in the pro-abortion camp. Nowadays, in the West, salt poisoning has been largely replaced by dilation and evacuation, which is not dissimilar to the method of dilation and curettage, except that dismemberment replaces any attempt at suction.

The fourth method, which is used for more developed pregnancies, is the hysterotomy. This is like a Caesarean operation, except that in the hysterotomy the object is not to save the child but to kill him. In this case, the baby has to be either killed outright or allowed to die. From time to time, the general public experiences some disquiet about such a practice. In January, 1969 an unmarried student in Glasgow was aborted of a twenty-six-weeks-old baby. The little infant was placed in a bag and handed to the incinerator attendant. Half-an-hour later the attendant heard a whimper coming from the bag. Vigorous attempts were then made to try to save the child, but these failed and the child died some eight hours later.[6]

A fifth method must now be discussed. This is referred to as a partial-birth abortion. It is designed to kill a viable child. The unborn baby is rotated in the womb so as to be born feet first. As the feet emerge, the abortionist pierces the baby's skull in order to suction out the brains. The head of the baby is kept inside the mother so as to maintain the pretence that the process is not murder. In fact, the procedure shows the minimal difference that exists between abortion and infanticide. When a conscience is evil (*Heb.* 10:22) or seared (*1 Tim.* 4:2), semantics become a refuge—albeit a delusional one.

In the United States, President Bill Clinton twice vetoed Congressional attempts to outlaw partial-birth abortions, but even ardent supporters of abortion were uneasy. Janet Hadley admits that 'Late abortions represent a wafer-thin line between the tolerable and the intolerable, the merely disturbing and the truly revolting.'[7] They are not uncommon. In January 2000 at the Royal Women's Hospital, Melbourne, Australia, a child of 32 weeks was aborted in January 2000 because the mother was told the child could have had dwarfism. It emerged that the hospital routinely performed about 30-40 late abortions (i.e. after 20 weeks) each year.[8] Six months later we were reassured

[6] Cited in R. F. R. Gardner, *Abortion: the Personal Dilemma* (Exeter: Paternoster, 1975), pp. 84-85.

[7] J. Hadley, *Abortion: Between Freedom and Necessity* (London: Virago Press, 1996), p. 68.

[8] *Sydney Morning Herald,* 30 November, 2000.

by an interim report that the medical staff had all acted in good faith.[9] Finally, in the USA in 2007 the practice of partial-birth abortion was outlawed, although this ban is still very much under threat. The *New York Times,* for example, continued to defend the indefensible, and asserted that this procedure should be allowed on the bizarre ground that it was 'an issue so vital to women's privacy and health.'[10]

Despite the worst efforts of doctors, a number of babies have survived abortions. Possibly some 500 to 1,000 abortions are born alive each year in the USA.[11] Almost 1% of all abortions—that is, about 40 each working day—are performed after the 22nd week.[12] On 14 July, 1998 in Darwin, Australia a baby girl survived for 80 minutes after being aborted. The baby was supposed to be 19 weeks' old, and the mother had been given drugs to induce an abortion. During the night of 13-14 July she gave birth to a daughter who exhibited encouraging vital life signs. A registered mid-wife was shocked when she heard the little girl cry, and felt herself in the midst of what she called 'a very big moral dilemma'—having come to work expecting to preside over a stillbirth, she was faced with a live infant. The doctor experienced no such moral dilemma, and denied any doctor-patient relationship with the infant.[13]

---

[9] *Sydney Morning Herald,* 12 July, 2000; *The Australian,* 12 July, 2000.

[10] The *New York Times,* 11 November, 2006. President Clinton's slogan was that he wanted to make abortion 'safe, legal and rare'. In 1946 George Orwell complained that 'Political language . . . is designed to make lies sound truthful and murder respectable, and to give an appearance of solidity to pure wind' (cf. Orwell's essay, 'Politics and the English Language').

[11] Marvin Olasky, *The Press and Abortion, 1838-1988* (New Jersey: Lawrence Erlbaum Associates, 1988), pp. 131-132.

[12] Francis Beckwith, *Politically Correct Death* (Michigan: Baker, 1993), p. 34.

[13] Coroners Court at Darwin in the Northern Territory of Australia, An Inquest into the Death of Jessica Jane (name suppressed), no. 9815022, delivered 10 April, 2000.

There were eight abortion survivors at the Eleventh World Conference of Human Life International in May 1992, including Gianna Jessen.[14] On 24 October, 2006 in Miami, Florida, a premature baby, Amillia Taylor, was born. She was aged only 21 weeks and 6 days, and was slightly longer than a ballpoint pen in length. Yet four months later she was strong enough to be taken home.[15] Such is the moral state of the West—premature babies are surviving while those of the same age are being aborted; and to complicate the picture a small minority of the abortions survive.

So far as the genetic code is concerned, the normal baby has all forty-six chromosomes at conception. His heart is beating at twenty days, and at six weeks brain waves can be detected. About this time hiccoughs can occur. He has all his organs by the time he is eight weeks old, and by about twelve or thirteen weeks he recoils from pain and sucks his thumb. Dr Paul Rockwell of New York has described a two-months-old foetus who was aborted due to a ruptured ectopic pregnancy. The tiny boy, only one centimetre long, was swimming in the amniotic fluid in the embryo sac. In Dr Rockwell's words:

> The tiny human was perfectly developed, with long tapering fingers, feet and toes. It was almost transparent, as regards the skin, and the delicate arteries and veins were prominent to the ends of the fingers. The baby was extremely alive and swam about the sac approximately one time per second, with a natural swimmer's stroke . . . When the sac was opened, the tiny human immediately lost its life.[16]

[14] See Jessica Shaver, *Gianna* (Colorado: Focus on the Family, 1995).

[15] *Sydney Morning Herald,* 21 February, 2007.

[16] Cited in 'Pro-Life News', *Right to Life Newsletter,* NSW, Vol. 2, no. 14, October, 1980.

The differences between a baby before birth and a baby after birth lie in the areas of physical maturity and geographical location. There is a continuity in life, beginning at conception, and it is arbitrary to say life begins at animation, viability or birth. As dramatic as birth is, it is not magical; the baby is not wonderfully transformed from a blob of foetal tissue into a human being; from the beginning it was a human being who was conceived. We are all, in the graphic words of Paul Ramsey, 'fellow fetuses'.[17]

It is sometimes said that we cannot know when the foetus becomes a human being. In fact, the Supreme Court of the United States maintained just this view in its momentous and tragic decision of 1973 when it virtually allowed abortion on demand. The Court stated: 'We need not resolve the difficult question of when life begins.' It then went on to imply that issues of theological, philosophical, and biological speculation have no place in a court of law. Such a statement gives the appearance of humility, but it flies in the face of biological reality. Even if it were true, the Court's cavalier attitude to life gives grave cause for alarm. If there is any uncertainty as to when life begins, the duty of the Court is surely to protect what, on the Court's own admission, might be human life. After all, this same Court would hardly exonerate a man who fired a gun into a house if he entered the plea that he thought the house might have been empty. The attitude of the distinguished surgeon, Dr C. Everett Koop, is a most worthy one: 'I recognize full well the chance for errors in judgment. Because of that I try to err only on the side of life.'[18]

---

[17] P. Ramsey in John T. Noonan (ed), *The Morality of Abortion* (Massachusetts: Harvard University Press, 1970), p. 67.

[18] C. Everett Koop, *The Right to Live: the Right to Die* (Illinois: Tyndale, 1976), p. 117.

The practice of abortion is by no means uniquely modern. It is referred to in Middle Assyrian literature, and both Plato and Aristotle gave qualified approval to it. By the time of the Roman Empire, it was widely accepted, and thus had to be confronted head-on by the expanding Christian Church. This confrontation was so successful that the sanctity of unborn life attained what John T. Noonan has called 'an almost absolute value' in European history.[19] This is not to say that abortions never happened; references to it appear in many places, both likely and unlikely. Tolstoy's wife, a woman of conventional Russian Orthodox views, once tried to abort one of her babies.[20] In general, however, support for practices like abortion and infanticide was confined to those outside the mainstream of European thought. The Marquis de Sade, the patron saint of cruelty, was one such advocate.

In modern times, abortion has been championed in revolutionary Russia. In 1934, for example, there were three times as many abortions as births in Moscow hospitals.[21] The State was naturally alarmed at this situation, and in 1935 tightened up its liberal abortion laws. Later it relaxed them again, to the point where one report in 1981 even claimed that the average woman in the USSR had six abortions during her lifetime.[22] The Soviet regime was never noted for the high value it placed on human life and dignity, but first Japan, then Eastern Europe and finally the West followed its lead in allowing, even promoting, the practice of abortion. Abortion has thus become so much accepted in places like Britain, the United States, and Australia, that one child out

[19] John Noonan, 'An Almost Absolute Value in History' in J. T. Noonan (ed.), *The Morality of Abortion* (Massachusetts: Harvard University Press, 1970).

[20] H. Troyat, *Tolstoy* (Victoria: Penguin, 1970), p. 611.

[21] Cited in O. R. Johnston, *Who Needs the Family?* (London: Hodder and Stoughton, 1979), p. 28.

[22] *Time,* 6 April, 1981, p. 23.

of every three or four conceived is deliberately put to death in the womb. The statistics have indeed become horrifying. In the United States, for example, up to 1,500,000 abortions have taken place each year since 1973—about three every minute—although this number started to decline towards the end of the twentieth century. Each year some 190,000 abortions are performed in England and Wales and up to 100,000 in Australia. On the basis of these figures it is calculated that the number of babies killed in the USA through abortion in four months is approximately equal to the number of Americans killed during the whole of World War II. In the civilized West the womb has become more deadly than the battlefield.

Yet all this has taken place in the name of care and compassion, complete with the touching catch-cry, 'Every child a wanted child'. It is not altogether unlike the situation described in Orwell's *Nineteen-Eighty-Four* where the Ministry of Love runs the secret police and the Ministry of Truth is in charge of propaganda. The words of Isaiah from the eighth century B.C. now take on new meaning: 'Woe to those who call evil good, and good evil; who substitute darkness for light and light for darkness; who substitute bitter for sweet, and sweet for bitter!' (*Isa.* 5:20). It is not that people have deliberately set out to promote evil, but rather, as Blaise Pascal put it, 'We never do evil so fully and cheerfully as when we do it out of conscience.'[23] Modern humanists no longer deviate from an accepted standard; it has become increasingly true that there is no longer any standard from which to deviate. To return to the eighth century B.C. again, the prophet Amos had a plumb-line by which he could judge Israel (*Amos* 7:7-9), but modern secular man has been left

[23] Pascal, *Pensées* (Victoria: Penguin, 1973), translated by A. J. Krailsheimer, p. 272.

without any plumb-line. As a result, in the abortion debate, he has not simply come up with the wrong answers; he has been unable even to frame the right questions.

2. Is There A Standard
in Ethics?

A mos used the image of a plumb-line, but the great French scientist and Christian thinker, Blaise Pascal, wrote of a ship drawing away from the shore. To the people on the ship, it appears as though the shore is moving, but to those on the shore, it is the ship that is moving. Pascal then asks, 'Where are we going to find a harbour in morals?'[24] That is the question. Can we find a standard by which to judge all other standards? Secular humanism claims that there is no such standard; it answers with Jean-Jacques Rousseau: 'Whatever I feel to be right is right. Whatever I feel to be wrong is wrong.'[25] When this is translated into civil legislation, it tends to be along the lines suggested by the dictum coined by Mrs Patrick Campbell and popularized by Joseph Fletcher: 'People can do what they want as long as they don't do it in the streets and frighten the horses.'[26] John Stuart Mill would have put it more elegantly, but essentially that is the position of many in the Western democracies in the twentieth century.

[24] Pascal, *op. cit.,* p. 247.
[25] Cited in N. Hampson, *The Enlightenment* (Penguin, 1968), p. 195.
[26] J. Fletcher, *Situation Ethics* (London: SCM, 1978), p. 140.

Janet Hadley cites one woman who wanted an abortion because she was going on a skiing holiday, but then adds: 'Dividing reasons for abortion into "good" and "bad" is a treacherous moral enterprise.' She asks: 'How can anyone make such moral judgments?'[27] It is strange, but such reasoning is usually only applied to matters like abortion and sexual ethics, not racism and paedophilia.

Tragically, much of the professing Church has capitulated to just such an outlook. Situation ethics is widely held, leading to the conviction that nothing can be labelled 'wrong' except lack of love.[28] Joseph Fletcher quotes Paul Tillich's assertion that 'The law of love is the ultimate law because it is the negation of law',[29] and claims that this is the Christian approach to ethics. Augustine's saying, 'Love, and do what you will',[30] has also become popular, although, understood in Fletcher's sense, it is by no means an accurate summary of Augustine's own approach to ethics.[31] In any case, Fletcher's views are a distortion of biblical teaching on ethics; the Scriptures everywhere assume and teach that the moral law is permanent and binding. Both Testaments affirm that love and law go together, each giving meaning to the other. Sin is never portrayed simply as an offence against the inner glow of love, but as lawlessness (*1 John* 3:4). Where there is no law, neither is there any violation (*Rom.* 4:15). No doubt, Adam and Eve sinned against love, but basically they sinned against God's law (*Gen.* 2:16-17).

---

[27] J. Hadley, *Abortion: Between Freedom and Necessity* (London: Virago Press, 1996), pp. 79-80.

[28] Cf. J. A. T. Robinson, *Honest to God* (London: SCM, 1964), pp. 116-118.

[29] Fletcher, *op. cit.,* p. h (unnumbered).

[30] From Augustine's *Sermons on the Epistles of John,* VII 8.

[31] Cf. e.g. Augustine's *On Lying.*

The Old Testament teaches that loving God is linked with keeping his commandments (*Deut.* 6:5-9; 10:12; 11:1; 30:16). Loving the Lord means obeying his voice (*Deut.* 30:20). Obviously, one can abuse the law, as Jezebel did the law against blasphemy (*1 Kings* 21:1-16), so the law cannot guarantee morality. But nowhere do we find love opposing the law. In the Psalms, love and law go together (e.g. *Psa.* 40:). In Psalm 119, the psalmist says ten times that he loves God's law. Jeremiah saw that believers would have God's law in their hearts (*Jer.* 31:33), meaning that it would be inwritten, not unwritten. Ezekiel also taught that when God's Spirit is within us, we walk in his statutes and are careful to observe his ordinances (*Ezek.* 36:27). The Old Testament knows nothing of the dichotomy which places the Spirit, love and freedom on one side, and the chains of the law on the other. As the Psalmist says, 'I will keep thy law continually, for ever and ever. And I will walk at liberty, for I seek thy precepts' (*Psa.* 119:44-45).

Naturally, since God is the author of both Testaments, we find the same teaching in the New Testament. Jesus set his face against the traditions of the Pharisees, and he drew out the full meaning of the law, but he never pitted his authority against the law of God as recorded in the Old Testament (*Matt.* 5:17-20). Three times in John 14, Jesus makes obedience to his commands the test of a disciple's love (*John* 14:15, 21, 23). In order to reinforce this, our Lord repeated this teaching in John 15:10. The Lord Jesus taught that the law and the prophets rest upon the love of God and man (*Matt.* 22: 40); he did not teach that love renders the law and the prophets obsolete.

The same teaching can be found in the Apostle Paul. Paul makes it clear that the law cannot bring salvation to sinful man (*Rom.* 3:9-20), and that, so far as salvation is concerned, a Christian is not under the law (*Rom.* 6:14; 7:1-3; *Gal.* 5:18). Yet Paul still claimed that he was not nullifying the law but establishing it (*Rom.* 3:31). For Paul, as for Jesus, love fulfils the law (*Rom.* 13: 8, 10); it does not abolish it (*Rom.* 13:9). In short, Paul delighted in the law (*Rom.* 7: 22). It is very instructive to compare passages such as 1 Corinthians 7:19, Galatians 5:6, and Galatians 6:15. In each of these passages, Paul declares that neither circumcision nor uncircumcision matters. What is important is the keeping of God's commandments (*1 Cor.* 7:19), faith working through love (*Gal.* 5:6), and a new creation (*Gal.* 6:15). It is evident that Paul considered keeping the law and faith working through love as complementary rather than antithetical.

The Apostle John likewise maintains that the love of God in a Christian will lead to his keeping of the commandments (*1 John* 2:3-5; 3:21-23). The 'apostle of love' writes that 'this is the love of God, that we keep his commandments' (*1 John* 5:3). Similarly, when James refers to 'the law of liberty', he does not mean liberty from obedience to the law, but the liberty to be 'an effectual doer' (*James* 1:25). It is clear that our Lord and the apostles did not see love as just a warm feeling of general benevolence, but saw it as including faithful obedience to all of God's precepts.

The modern age has absolutized concepts like love, freedom and happiness, but in divorcing these from God's command-ments, it has necessarily distorted them. J. G. Machen has vividly illustrated this in his story of the drunkard armed with the Golden Rule that one should do unto others as one would have others do to oneself (*Matt.* 7:12). As Machen says, the drunkard will take this to mean that he should buy his friends another drink.[32] Another example might be found in Shakespeare's *Othello*

[32] J. G. Machen, *Christianity and Liberalism* (Michigan: Eerdmans, 1923, reprinted 1974), p. 37.

where Othello murders his wife Desdemona in a fit of unjustified jealousy. After the murder, Othello speaks of himself as 'one that lov'd not wisely but too well'.[33] Love, when separated from law, simply loses all meaning. Love and law were joined together by God; it is not for man to rend them asunder.

Modern man thinks of freedom in terms of the removal of all restraints, but this shallow approach must lead to man's self-destruction. Drawing from the wells of biblical truth, the Puritan Samuel Bolton saw clearly that 'If we claim to be free from obedience, we make ourselves the servants of sin.'[34] His fellow-Puritan William Perkins pointed out the positive side of the same truth: 'the service of God is not bondage, but perfect liberty.'[35] The Word of God warns against those who promise freedom while they themselves are slaves of corruption (2 Pet. 2:19). True freedom is to be found in being a slave to righteousness (Rom. 6). Situation ethics promises a false freedom which turns the grace of God into licentiousness (Jude 4).

The Bible thus gives no support to those who wish to relativize the moral law. Too often, the clash between Jesus and the Pharisees is portrayed as a clash between love and law, but this is a false antithesis. It must be stressed, however, that Christian ethics cannot be maintained simply by giving people the law of God. The law by itself has no power to confer righteousness upon sinful man; rather, it only condemns him (Rom. 3:20; 7:7-9; Gal. 3:10). Christian ethics derive their power from God's grace in Christ and the outpouring of his Spirit. That is why the great Thomas Chalmers declared that 'to preach Christ is the only effective way

---

[33] *Othello,* Act v, Scene II.

[34] S. Bolton, *The True Bounds of Christian Freedom* (Edinburgh: Banner of Truth, 1645, reprinted 1978), p. 58.

[35] Cited in E. F. Kevan, *The Grace of Law* (Michigan: Guardian Press, 1976), p. 248.

of preaching morality'.[36] Christian doctrine and Christian ethics are wedded together. Insane as he was, Friedrich Nietzsche has proved himself more clear-headed on this point than many others who consider themselves more favourably disposed towards some form of Christian morality. Nietzsche wrote,

> When one gives up Christian belief one thereby deprives oneself of the right to Christian morality . . . Christianity is a system, a consistently thought out and complete view of things. If one breaks out of it a fundamental idea, the belief in God, one thereby breaks the whole thing to pieces: one has nothing of any consequence left in one's hands.'[37]

Nietzsche was simply saying what the Bible says—ethics requires doctrine as a necessary foundation. Doctrinal sections of Scripture are often followed by sections on ethics, and linked by the word 'therefore' (e.g., *Rom.* 12:1; *Eph.* 4:1; *Heb.* 10:19). Paul well realized that if the doctrine of the resurrection is not true, then Christian ethics cannot last (*1 Cor.* 15:32). Similarly, Peter's call for holiness in 2 Peter 3:14-18 is based on the fact that Christ will come again and judge the world (*2 Pet.* 3:1-13). All this means that the revival of Christian ethical practice largely depends on a revival of faith in Christ and his Word. Apart from him, we can do nothing (*John* 15: 5). Samuel Bolton has a most succinct summary: 'The law sends us to the Gospel for our justification; the Gospel sends us to the law to frame our way of life.'[38]

Hence, there is indeed a harbour in morals—this is the law of God. The law by itself is not enough to inculcate morality; it is the Spirit who gives God's people power to fulfil his law (*Ezek.* 36:26-27; *Rom.* 8:13), and the Spirit is only given to

[36] T. Chalmers, *Collected Works,* Vol. 12 (Glasgow, 1838-42), p. 110.

[37] Cited in C. Chapman, *The Case for Christianity* (England: Lion, 1981), p. 188.

[38] S. Bolton, *The True Bounds of Christian Freedom,* p. 72.

those who have faith in Christ (*John* 7:37-39). But since we have a standard by which to judge all other standards, the next question must be: Does the Bible give us any guidelines on the matter of abortion?

3. ABORTION IN THE LIGHT OF GOD'S WORD

It is frequently contended that the Bible says next to nothing on the subject of abortion. R. F. R. Gardner even goes so far as to state that there is 'no clear-cut Scriptural guidance' on abortion.[39] This is not altogether accurate. It is true that the Bible says nothing directly on the subject of abortion—anymore than it speaks directly on computer hacking and nuclear war—but we do well to remember the important principle laid down by the *Westminster Confession of Faith:* 'The whole counsel of God concerning all things necessary for his glory, man's salvation, faith and life, is either expressly set down in Scripture, or by good and necessary consequence may be deduced from Scripture' [I, VI]. On these premises, it is certainly possible to derive the biblical attitude to abortion.

In the Bible, conception is regarded as a precious gift from God, the giver of life (e.g. *Gen.* 4:1, 25; 21:1ff; 25:21; 29:31-35; 30:17-24; 33:5; *Deut.* 7:13; 28:4; *Judg.* 13:2-7; *Ruth* 4:13; *1 Sam.* 1:1-20; *Psa.* 113:9; 127:3-5; 128:1-6; *Isa.* 54:1; *Luke* 1:24; *1 Tim.* 2:15). God as the creator is the source of life, and to choose God is to choose life (*Deut.* 30:15, 19-20).

[39] R. F. R. Gardner, *op. cit.,* p. 254.

Given that background, the most obvious starting point for treatment of abortion must be Exodus 21:22-25, although Joe Sprinkle has warned that it is 'ill suited for establishing a biblical ethic concerning abortion'.[40] This text is not without ambiguities, and can be interpreted in two possible ways. The first interpretation can be found in the New American Standard Bible:

> And if men struggle with each other and strike a woman with child so that she has a miscarriage, yet there is no further injury, he shall surely be fined as the woman's husband may demand of him; and he shall pay as the judges decide. But if there is any further injury, then you shall appoint as a penalty life for life, eye for eye, tooth for tooth, hand for hand, foot for foot, burn for burn, wound for wound, bruise for bruise.

A similar interpretation is given by the RSV, the New English Bible and the Good News Bible, as well as by the commentators Brevard Childs and R. A. Cole.

If this is the correct translation, it would appear to justify the view that the mother's life is of greater value than that of the unborn child. The unborn child would then be viewed as nascent life rather than as a full human being.[41] However, even this translation does not open the door to abortion but precludes it. Here, an accidental abortion leads to a fine. 'Good and necessary' deduction would entail that deliberate abortion warrants a much heavier punishment. At most, this view of Exodus 21:

---

[40] J. M. Sprinkle, 'The Interpretation of Exodus 21:22-25 (Lex Talionis) and Abortion' in Westminster Theological Journal, 55, 1993, p. 253.

[41] This is Helmut Thielicke's view; cf. The Ethics of Sex (Cambridge: James Clarke and Co., 1978), pp. 243-7. Joe Sprinkle and Robert Congdon consider that the more likely view is that the unborn child dies (J. Sprinkle, 'The Interpretation of Exodus 21:22-25 (Lex Talionis) and Abortion' in Westminster Theological Journal, 55, 1993, pp. 233-253; and R. Congdon, 'Exodus 21:22-25 and the Abortion Debate' in Bibliotheca Sacra, vol. 146, no. 582, April-June 1989, p. 139).

22-25 might justify abortion in the now extremely rare case where the pregnancy seriously threatens the physical life of the mother. The point of the passage would then be the extraordinary protection given to the expectant mother—for manslaughter was not treated as a 'life for life' issue (*Josh.* 20)—not the lesser protection given to the baby.

The second interpretation, namely that Exodus 21 refers to the death of either mother or child, gains support from the translation of the Authorized Version, which is also followed by the New International Version and the English Standard Version. This says, 'If men strive, and hurt a woman with child, so that her fruit depart from her [the NIV says, 'she gives birth prematurely'], and yet no mischief [NIV says, 'serious injury'] follow: he shall be surely punished, according as the woman's husband will lay upon him; and he shall pay as the judges determine. And if any mischief follow, then thou shalt give life for life . . .'[42] On this translation, it is possible that the verses do not refer to a miscarriage, but to a premature birth. If the young infant survives, the guilty men are fined, but if he dies, it is life for life. In fact, the passage has been understood in this way by the learned Puritan exegete, Matthew Poole, and by Keil and Delitzsch, whose commentaries on the Old Testament have long been regarded as standard works of reference. Calvin's comments are also most instructive. The great Genevan Reformer wrote that 'the foetus, though enclosed in the womb of its mother, is already a human being'. Hence, he concluded that the passage referred to the possible death of either mother or child. He therefore protested vigorously against the murder of the unborn:

---

[42] It should be pointed out that the 'life for life' principle in practice often meant the payment of a ransom as a substitute (e.g. *Exod.* 21:29-30; *1 Kings* 20:39).

If it seems more horrible to kill a man in his own house than in a field, because a man's house is his place of most secure refuge, it ought surely to be deemed more atrocious to destroy a foetus in the womb before it has come to light.[43]

This second interpretation of Exodus 21:22-25 has not found widespread support today, although John Stott in 1984 regarded the first interpretation as 'gratuitous', and argued that 'It seems much more probable that the scale of penalty was to correspond to the degree of injury, whether to the mother or to her child, in which case mother and child are valued equally.'[44] There is indeed much to be said in favour of this view. In the first place, the Hebrew word for 'miscarriage' is not used in the passage, although it can be found in other parts of the Old Testament (e.g. *Gen.* 31:38; *Hos.* 9:14). Instead, Exodus 21:22 uses a word which simply means 'to depart' or 'to go out'. It is used, for example, to describe Abram's departure from Haran in Genesis 12:4. It is also used to describe live births (e.g. *Gen.* 25:26; 38: 28-30). Admittedly, it is used of a stillborn infant in Numbers 12:12, but one can only repeat that the modern translations which insert the word 'miscarriage' into the text are interpreting rather than translating.

The second reason for accepting that Exodus 21 refers to the death of either mother or child is more compelling. The Scriptures, as the Word of God, consistently refer to the unborn child as a human being. Every child in the womb is fearfully and wonderfully made by God (*Job* 31:15; *Psa.* 139:13-16; *Isa.* 44: 2, 24; *Jer.* 1:5), in a way that we can never completely understand (*Eccles.* 11:5). There is a continuity in life, from conception to

[43] J. Calvin, *Commentaries on the Last Four Books of Moses,* Vol. 3, translated by C. W. Bingham (Michigan: Baker, reprinted 1979), pp. 41-42.
[44] J. Stott, *Issues Facing Christians Today* (Hants: Marshall Morgan & Scott, 1984), p. 289.

death, so naturally when David refers to his origins in the womb, he uses the first-person personal pronoun (*Psa.* 139:13). Even sin is traced back, not to the newborn baby, but to the unborn infant (*Psa.* 51:5; 58:3). As a result, the unborn are always treated in Scripture as human—they can move, even leap (*Gen.* 25:22; *Luke* 1:41, 44), be consecrated in God's service (*Jer.* 1:5; *Gal.* 1:15), filled with the Holy Spirit (*Luke* 1:15), and blessed (*Luke* 1: 42). Furthermore, the same Greek word is used to describe the unborn John the Baptist (*Luke* 1: 41, 44), the newborn baby Jesus (*Luke* 2:12, 16) and the young children who were brought to Jesus (*Luke* 18: 15). If the unborn child is not a human being, it is difficult to see how these statements could have any meaning. And it is surely significant that when the eternal Son of God became Man, he entered Mary's womb. The incarnation, the union of the divine with the human, must be dated from the conception, not the birth, of our Lord. God became an embryo!

Since the unborn child is a live human being, it is therefore possible for him to die in the womb (cf. *Job* 10:18). The Apostle Paul could even refer to himself as an abortion—an abortion who lived (*1 Cor.* 15:8). When the prophet Jeremiah broke out into that remarkable cry of despondency in Jeremiah 20, he cursed the day of his birth, and went on to curse the man who could have killed him in his mother's womb, but did not (*Jer.* 20:14-18). Had the prophet lived in modern Western society, he might have had his wish fulfilled! The unnamed recipient of Jeremiah's curse was guilty, in Jeremiah's jaundiced eyes, 'because he did not kill me in the womb, so that my mother became my grave' (*Jer.* 20:17). The word that is used here to describe the killing of a child in the womb is the same word that is used to describe David's slaying of Goliath in 1 Samuel 17:50-51. Apparently, Jeremiah knew of no euphemism such as 'termination of pregnancy'.

Throughout Scripture, God's judgment always falls on those who slay the unborn. The prophet Elisha wept when he thought of the crimes that Hazael, the king of Syria, would commit against Israel. In Elisha's words, 'their little ones you will dash in pieces, and their women with child you will rip up' (*2 Kings* 8:11-12). Later, the same evil was perpetuated by Menahem, one of Israel's last kings (*2 Kings* 15:16). When the heathen Ammonites ripped open the pregnant women of Gilead, the prophet Amos declared that God's judgment lay close at hand (*Amos* 1:13). All this indicates that, contrary to some claims, God's Word does give clear-cut guidelines on the subject of abortion.

The biblical injunctions against child sacrifice are also not without relevance for the abortion debate. God did not allow the Israelites to enter Canaan until the iniquity of the Amorites was complete (*Gen.* 15:16). As Canaanite culture became more debased, God prepared the Israelites to take possession of the promised land. Repeatedly, God warned the Israelites not to imitate their heathen neighbours (e.g., *Lev.* 18:24-30; 20:23). One of the things that God especially warned against was the sacrificial offering of children through fire to the Ammonite god Molech (*Lev.* 18:21; 20:2-5; *Deut.* 12:31; 18:10). However, as early as Solomon's reign, the worship of Molech was taking place in Israel (*1 Kings* 11:7). The practice of child sacrifice soon spread to Moab (*2 Kings* 3:27), and even to Judah where Ahaz in the eighth century B.C. (*2 Kings* 16:3; *2 Chron.* 28:3) and Manasseh in the seventh century B.C. (*2 Kings* 21:6, *2 Chron.* 33:6) were guilty of the crime. In 722 B.C. the northern kingdom of Israel was destroyed by the Assyrians, partly because of Israel's participation in this brutal and idolatrous practice (*2 Kings* 17:17; cf. *Psa.* 106:34-39).

These child sacrifices prompted the prophets to declare God's judgment upon his people and to command repentance. Isaiah and later Jeremiah and Ezekiel were particularly moved to denounce the worship of Molech (see *Isa.* 57:5; *Jer.* 7:31; 1:4-5; 32:35; *Ezek.* 16:20-21; 20:31; 23:37, 39). When God said that He would not hear the prayers of the Judeans because their hands were full of blood, it is likely that the child sacrifices were at least partly in mind (*Isa.* 1:15). Much later, as Jerusalem edged closer to disaster, the godly king Josiah tried to reform Judah according to God's law. Part of this reformation consisted of trying to abolish these sacrifices of children to Molech (*2 Kings* 23:10). It is indeed a sobering thought that the valley of Hinnom, to the south of Jerusalem, which was the site for these child sacrifices (see *2 Chron.* 33:6; *Jer.* 7:31), was later used by Jesus as a picture of hell (e.g., *Luke* 12:5). The word 'hell' or *'Gehenna'* comes from the Greek word *geenna* which in turn comes from the Hebrew *gê* ('valley of') *hinnōm ('Hinnom')*.

God's Word thus has much to say to us on the issue of abortion. Today, we see again Rachel, the woman of faith, weeping for her children because they are not (*Matt.* 2:18). Arguments in favour of abortion will also prove to be arguments in favour of euthanasia and infanticide—and hence a return to the practices of Pharaoh (*Exod.* 1) and Herod (*Matt.* 2:16-18). Those who hate God invariably love death (*Prov.* 8:36). Unborn life is indeed human life, and so embraced by God's commandment which forbids murder (*Exod.* 20:13). The cause of the unborn child is thus God's cause: 'Though my father and mother forsake me, the Lord will receive me' (*Psa.* 27:10, NIV).

One question might remain to be considered: What about the extreme case where an unborn child seriously threatens the physical life of the mother? This question is largely academic now. One occasionally hears of an ectopic pregnancy (i.e. where the child is not growing in the uterus but in the fallopian tubes). Here, an abortion is obviously necessary, in the present state of technology, as a developed pregnancy can only have one result—death for both mother and child. However, in the case where it appears that an unborn child in the womb is a threat to the mother's life, we can only reassert the biblical position that life begins at conception. Hence, Bonhoeffer's assertion that 'The question whether the life of the mother or the life of the child is of greater value can hardly be a matter for a human decision.'[45] The fallibility of human doctors, even on medical matters, is a further cause for hesitation. There have been numerous cases where doctors have warned a mother-to-be that an abortion was necessary to save her life, yet, in the end, both mother and child were brought safely through the whole trial.

In the light of the Bible's teaching on abortion, the stance of the Christian needs to be firm and decisive. The great Reformer Martin Luther warned against any temptation to compromise God's truth. Luther stated, 'If I profess with the loudest voice and clearest exposition every portion of the truth of God except precisely that little point which the world and the devil are at that moment attacking, I am not confessing Christ.' Timely words indeed!

---

[45] Bonhoeffer, *Ethics* p. 150 n. 1.

4. WOUNDED WOMEN

Advances in science have made it increasingly obvious that the unborn child is a human being. The normally pro-abortion *New Scientist* in March 2006 reported soberly:

The task force finds that the new recombinant DNA technologies indisputably prove that the unborn child is a whole human being from the moment of fertilization, that all abortions terminate the life of a living human being, and that the unborn child is a separate human patient under the care of modern medicine.

This naturally has implications for those who participate in abortion, and so the task force concluded:

It is simply unrealistic to expect that a pregnant mother is capable of being involved in the termination of the life of her child without risk of suffering significant psychological trauma and distress. To do so is beyond the normal, natural, and healthy capability of a woman whose natural instincts are to protect and nurture her child.[46]

The pro-abortion slogans of the 1960s and 1970s were always

[46] Alison Motluk, 'Abortion: Science, politics and morality collide' in *New Scientist,* issue no. 2543, 18 March 2006, pp. 8-9.

fanciful and dangerous. Reality has started to strike home in the most unexpected places.

In 1996 David Reardon argued that abortion harms women, and therefore the pro-life movement needs to change the focus of the abortion debate so it concentrates on the issue of defending the interests of women.[47] In Reardon's view, a pro-life, pro-woman strategy will lead to the disintegration of the abortion industry. In martial arts, one uses the momentum of one's opponent to one's own advantage, and Reardon believes that the pro-life movement must learn what he calls 'the art of cultural judo'.[48] He distinguishes between those who are pro-abortion and those who are more ambivalently pro-choice. Since abortion not only destroys the life of the baby but also the well-being of the mother, a cogent argument against abortion can be mounted based on the welfare of the mother.

Reardon's approach has much to commend it, although the fact that every abortion involves the deliberate killing of a child must remain the most heinous aspect of the operation. Abortion is an issue of morality before it is an issue of pain. Nevertheless, evidence has mounted to show that abortion has a devastating impact on the woman who aborts her child. Sin alienates us from God, from each other, and from ourselves. Grief, depression, anxiety, thought of suicide, and destructive behaviour in terms of drugs, alcohol, and promiscuity are consequences that are all too common yet all too rarely faced by a society addicted to the gods of pleasure and convenience—idols whose promises are delusions and whose service is bondage.

[47] D. Reardon, *Making Abortion Rare* (Illinois: Acorn Books, 1996). See John Leland, 'Some Abortion Foes Forgo Politics for Quiet Talk', in the *New York Times,* 16 January 2006. In the Australian context, this has been taken further by John Fleming and Nicholas Tonti-Filippini (eds), *Common Ground?* (Strathfield: St Pauls Publications, 2007).

[48] D. Reardon, *Making Abortion Rare* (Illinois: Acorn Books, 1996), p. 132.

Because the law of God is written upon the hearts of each one of us, and our consciences testify to this (*Rom.* 2:14-16), we ought not to be surprised that abortion, in killing the child, also damages the woman. After his adultery with Bathsheba and his murder, by proxy, of Uriah, David was so listless that he felt that his bones were wasting away, and his strength was dried up as in the heat of summer because God's hand was heavy upon him (*Psa.* 32:3-4). Anne Speckhard and Vincent Rue have written of what they call 'Postabortion Syndrome' as 'an emerging public health concern'.[49] In Britain in March 2008 the Royal College of Psychiatrists significantly modified a 1994 finding that the risks to mental health associated with continuing an unwanted pregnancy far outweighed the risks of regret over the abortion. Increasingly, even secular agencies were warning that abortion is linked with breakdowns in mental health.[50]

There is obvious unease in Western society over its mass killing of the smallest and most defenceless human beings. In 2004 in Perth, Australia an abortion clinic lodged an objection against a proposed child-care centre next door. The sight of children playing might well have upset some potential clients, and not

---

[49] Anne C. Speckhard and Vincent M. Rue, 'Postabortion Syndrome: An Emerging Public Health Concern' in *Journal of Social Issues*, vol. 48, no. 3, pp. 96, 103, 111, 112. See too D. Reardon, *Aborted Women Silent No More* (Illinois: Crossway, 1987); and David M. Fergusson, L. John Horwood, and Elizabeth M. Ridder, 'Abortion in Young Women and Subsequent Mental Health' in *Journal of Child Psychology & Psychiatry*, vol. 47, no.1, 2006, pp. 16-24. Strangely enough, in 1989 Dr Everett Koop, though strongly pro-life, saw no conclusive evidence of post-abortion syndrome; see C. Everett Koop, 'The U.S. Surgeon General on the Health Effects of Abortion' in *Population and Development Review*, 15, no. 1, 1989, p. 174. Apparently, Koop privately thought that abortion did harm the woman in terms of her health and psychological well-being, but he maintained that abortion was fundamentally a moral, not a health, issue; cf. D. Reardon, 'Revisiting the "Koop Report"', 2000, from http:www/afterabortion.info/koop.html

[50] 'Royal College warns abortions can lead to mental illness', *The Sunday Times*, 16 March, 2008, from www.timesonline

been good for business. The dispute was apparently solved by the building of a two-metre brick fence between the two proper-ties.[51] The same year saw Julia Black (who had an abortion herself when she was 21, and whose father was the head of Marie Stopes International, Britain's largest abortion provider) release her docu-mentary *My Foetus,* which was shown in Britain and Australia. This showed images of abortion procedures at four, seven, ten, eleven, and twenty-one weeks. The president of the Australian Medical Association, Dr Bill Glasson, opposed the showing of the film, and was quoted as saying: 'I think that society will be sickened by it.'[52] Presumably, a documentary on heart surgery would not attract the same response. One can only wonder why the depiction of abortion attracted such outrage when the reality of it is so widely ignored.

As early as 1986 Pam Koerbel was referring to 'abortion's second victim', and was concluding that the woman never gets over her abortion.[53] Terry Selby reports: 'I've known them to break down and cry and writhe on the floor in agony.'[54] In 1995 two well-known literary figures, Naomi Wolf and Peter Carey—one female and one male—publicly expressed their regret over being involved in abortion, with Naomi Wolf even speaking of the need for some kind of atonement.[55] Some pro-abortionists became fearful, and Beatrice Faust tried to rally the troops: 'Feminists must hold the line at women's right to choose

[51] M. Devine, 'Abortion is science's grim story' in *Sydney Morning Herald,* 5 August, 2004.

[52] *Sydney Morning Herald,* 10-11 July, 2004.

[53] Pam Koerbel, *Abortion's Second Victim* (Wheaton: Victor Books, 1986), pp. 184-185. See too Jennifer Doe, *One Day I'll See You* (Eastbourne: Kingsway, 1991).

[54] Terry Selby with Marc Bockmon, *The Mourning After: Help for Postabortion Syndrome* (Michigan: Baker, 1990), p. 87.

[55] See Peter Carey, 'My Lasting Wish' in *The Australian Magazine,* 14-15 October, 1995; Naomi Wolf, 'Our Bodies, Our Souls' in *The New Republic,* 16 October 1995; also *Weekend Australian,* 7-8 October, and 14-15 October, 1995.

and not get sidetracked into arguing about the foetus.'[56] Her strident claims were sounding less convincing. As a woman who had three abortions, she asserted: 'For the foetuses, I felt—and feel—nothing.'[57] Ultimately, she resorts to clichés and platitudes: 'We must cultivate the grace to respect diversity of conscience in a pluralist society.'[58] Meanwhile, a British feminist, Amanda Platell, in 2007 expressed her horror at the scale of abortion in Britain since 1967, but maintained, rather lamely, that 'We support the principle of abortion, but abhor the way it has come to be so misused and abused by the current generation.'[59]

Qualms—indeed grief—over abortion are not reserved for those who would call themselves religious or Christian. The rock singer, Suzi Quatro, has wistfully recorded that her affair with a married man in the late 1960s led to her having an abortion. Her own words, both poignant and tragic, are: 'When I get to those golden gates (hopefully) this is the sin I will pay for. Not a day goes by that I don't think about who that baby would be now. Children are a gift.'[60] In a typically confused way, she proclaims, with regard to abortion, that 'right is right and wrong is wrong', but later adds: 'I believed in the right to do whatever I wanted to do regardless of gender. Still do.'[61] Either we accept God's justification of the ungodly on his terms or we devise our own justification of ourselves, on our terms.

Every human being works with a concept of right and wrong. This does not make us infallible nor does it save anyone, but it is

[56] Beatrice Faust, 'Abortion Distortion', in *Weekend Australian,* 4-5 November, 1995.

[57] Beatrice Faust, 'Pro-choice but not anti-life', in *Weekend Australian,* 21-22 October, 1995.

[58] Ibid.

[59] Amanda Platell, 'Why I, as a feminist, abhor how the abortion law has been so abused', *Daily Mail,* 10 September 2007 online.

[60] Suzi Quatro, *Unzipped* (London: Hodder & Stoughton, 2007), p. 61.

[61] http://www.theage.com.au/articles/2007/08/24/1187462449221.html

part of what it means to be created in the image of God. George Orwell was a man who increasingly groped towards the light and suffered for his stand for what is right and true. In his novel, *Keep the Aspidistra Flying,* first published in 1936, Rosemary, the girlfriend of the protagonist, Gordon Comstock, falls pregnant. The couple face the temptation that perhaps abortion might be a way out of their dilemma. Gordon, however, responds quickly: 'He knew then that it was a dreadful thing they had been contemplating—a blasphemy, if that word had any meaning.'[62] Gordon went off to the public library to consult a book on midwifery, and was strangely moved:

> Here was the poor ugly thing, no bigger than a gooseberry, that he had created by his heedless act. Its future, its continued existence perhaps, depended on him. Besides, it was a bit of himself—it was himself. Dare one dodge such a responsibility as that?[63]

The novel concludes with Gordon experiencing a sense of life and purpose through the movement of his unborn child in Rosemary's womb.[64]

One British woman lamented after her abortions: 'Abortion isn't a way out; it begins a process of destruction.'[65] An Australian woman who aborted her child at ten weeks wrote: 'The emotional pain was worse than the physical discomfort. The emptiness, the loneliness, the loss, the sadness.'[66] A freelance writer from

[62] George Orwell, *Keep the Aspidistra Flying* (London: Penguin, 1937, reprinted 2000), p. 253.

[63] G. Orwell, *op.cit.,* p. 261.

[64] G. Orwell, *op.cit.,* p. 277.

[65] Melanie Symonds, . . . *And Still They Weep: Personal Stories of Abortion* (SPUC Educational Research Trust, 1996), p. 19.

[66] Christine Routley, 'Tragedy and Healing: Christine's Story' in M. O'Donovan and J. Stuparich, *The Abortion Debate: Pro-Life Essays* (ACT Right to Life Association, 1994), p. 26.

Melbourne has written: 'I am not a Christian, or a right-to-lifer, but I do know that it was my baby that I killed.'[67] Another Australian, Melinda Tankard Reist, has gathered evidence from some 250 women whose experiences have been summarised in the work, *Giving Sorrow Words*—a title taken from *Macbeth*, IV:3.[68] This work is a catalogue of human misery.

Women who have abortions often take to drink, indulge in promiscuous behaviour, and have thoughts of suicide. Nightmares are common, as well as fantasising about the baby. One woman who describes herself as not religious wrote: 'Sometimes I open my arms and embrace the air.' Six years after her abortion, she was writing: 'In my mind, I have a son I cannot touch and cannot feed and who follows me about like a ghost.'[69]

Most chilling of all is the bitter statement of one woman who said that she laughed when she heard that the daughter of her abortionist had been murdered.[70]

One feminist thought that she would have no troubles, but found that 'My head said one thing; my heart said another.' She went on: 'Feminist trailblazer by day, emotional cripple by night, I often cried myself to sleep curled up in the corner of my lounge room.' Even after she became a Christian, she still faced eight lonely and sorrowful years before she began to cope, if not live.[71]

One woman spoke to her aborted child: 'I feel you must hate me, with a fiery anger, but can you let it lie in peace, because I

[67] Ginger Ekselman, 'A chance, perhaps, to heal long after a mother's traumatic choice' in *Sydney Morning Herald,* 19 July, 2004.

[68] Melinda Tankard Reist, *Giving Sorrow Words* (Sydney: Duffy and Snellgrove, 2000).

[69] M. T. Reist, *op. cit.,* pp. 48-50.

[70] M. T. Reist, *op. cit.,* pp. 189-190.

[71] M. T. Reist, *op. cit.'* pp. 171-175.

am so sorry.'[72] Another laments: 'Abortion is such a secret loss and there is nothing tangible to grieve for. There are no mementoes (*sic*), photos, memories to share, no grave to visit, nothing recognisable to anyone else. It all takes place in your imagination.'[73] This is the grief that women are not supposed to feel—indeed, they are meant to experience relief. It is also the grief which is perhaps the loneliest grief of all. In the words of one woman: 'I have terminated myself.'[74]

The propaganda of the so-called pro-choice lobby has proved to be dreadfully misleading and empty. Consent may be given, but it is hardly informed. Hence abortion counselling is dismissed by one woman as 'bulldozing'.[75] There is only the appearance of choice, not the reality. Doctors often try to maintain the pretence that 'It's not a baby! It's a piece of foetus!'[76] Deep inside her heart the woman knows better. Abortion has indeed proved to be a war on women as well as a war on the unborn child.

It is a common experience amongst women that the loss of a child through miscarriage leads to grief, and even at times to a misplaced sense of guilt. Adrienne Ryan cites many parents who have, like her, suffered the loss of children through miscarriage. Without any Christian convictions, Mrs Ryan felt aggrieved when, while undergoing a miscarriage, she was placed in a hospital ward next to women seeking abortions.[77] She notes the comment of one man: 'Never make the cruel mistake of assuming that, just because the baby was not yet born, the pain is any less

[72] M. T. Reist, *op. cit.,* p. 151.

[73] M. T. Reist, *op. cit.,* p. 103.

[74] M. T. Reist, *op. cit.,* p. 230.

[75] M. T. Reist, *op. cit.,* p. 182.

[76] M. T. Reist, *op. cit.,* p. 134.

[77] A. Ryan, *A Silent Love* (Ringwood: Penguin, 2000), pp. 13-14.

than with any other loss.'[78] If that is the case with miscarriage, how much deeper is the pain associated with abortion where grief is compounded by guilt.

One of the most devastating indictments of abortion has actually come from the pen of a woman who spent her life defending the practice and participating in it. With her husband, Dr Bertram Wainer (who died in 1987), Mrs Jo Wainer opened what was euphemistically called a Fertility Control Clinic in East Melbourne in 1972. In 2006 Jo Wainer published some stories that were mainly—although not entirely—accounts of illegal abortions. Rather aptly the title she chose for the collection was *Lost*.[79] Rather less aptly the *Sydney Morning Herald* in March 2006 eulogised Dr Wainer as 'The man who saved women'![80]

The ostensible aim of the book is to defend the need for legal abortion, but it is like the proverbial boatman who faces one way and rows the other. Mrs Wainer claims that there were 90,000 illegal abortions each year in Australia—only slightly below the number of legal abortions at the present time.[81] This is designed to leave the reader with the impression that it is pointless to make abortion a criminal offence as the number of abortions remains largely constant. However, the true figure was well under 10,000. If Mrs Wainer plays up the number of illegal abortions, she plays down the significance of each abortion, asserting, without obvious relevance, that 'Abortion is a small word of only three syllables.'[82]

---

[78] A. Ryan, *op.cit.,* p. 63.

[79] Jo Wainer (ed), *Lost: Illegal Abortion Stories* (Carlton: Melbourne University Press, 2006).

[80] Fenella Souter, 'The man who saved women', in *Sydney Morning Herald,* Good Weekend, 25 March, 2006, pp. 20-25.

[81] Jo Wainer (ed), *op. cit.,* p. 2.

[82] Jo Wainer (ed), *op. cit.,* p. 3.

Unwittingly, it seems, Jo Wainer reveals how inherently de-humanizing is the practice of abortion. One woman, who had an illegal abortion in 1953, writes unblushingly: 'I certainly had no guilty feelings as I do not and never have liked or wanted a child, and never had any. I regard having the abortion, all things considered, to be the best thing I have ever done.'[83] It is the sort of argument that Josef Stalin might have used. The evil is undisguised. The woman has not even tried to pretend nobility. She both illustrates and denies Alexander Solzhenitsyn's insight: 'To do evil a human being must first of all believe that what he's doing is good, or else that it's a well-considered act in conformity with natural law.'[84]

Another woman is quite emphatic: 'I hate children. I especially hate babies.'[85] When she aborted her child at twenty weeks, her rage knew no bounds: 'I should have made sure it was dead. I should have torn it apart with my own bare hands, wreaking my vengeance upon it for what it did to me.'[86] One defence was: 'Animals leave their babies if they're weak, debilitated, or some way malformed. It's the survival of the fittest thing.'[87] These essays do not make for comforting reading. One woman laments: 'I felt putrid. I felt as low as anyone could ever get.'[88] These are stories of guilt, grief, callousness, fantasy, and almost unbounded sorrow.

Thus it is that the child is not the only casualty, nor the woman. Relationships rarely survive an abortion—about 80% of couples

[83] Jo Wainer (ed), *op. cit.,* p. 32.

[84] Alexander Solzhenitzyn, *The Gulag Archipelago,* vol. 1, translated by Thomas P. Whitney (Glasgow: Collins/Fontana, 1974) p. 173.

[85] Jo Wainer (ed), *op. cit.,* p. 72.

[86] Jo Wainer (ed), *op. cit.,* p. 88.

[87] Jo Wainer (ed), *op. cit.,* pp. 106-7.

[88] Jo Wainer (ed), *op. cit.,* p. 190.

break up after an abortion.[89] In so many cases, abortion is meant to save relationships but instead it destroys them. Jo Wainer records one woman who raged against her boyfriend's total lack of care, that 'he couldn't bear to be in the same room as me when I came back from the doctor's room.'[90] One woman married, then divorced her boyfriend after the abortion, and concluded that there were problems of unresolved guilt, bitterness and blame: 'The experience degraded us both.'[91] Hatred for one's husband or boyfriend is not uncommon.[92]

Indeed, abortion has a degrading effect on all involved in it,[93] despite the earnest efforts of those committed to the view that it is an operation no different to any other medical operation.[94] A kind of schizophrenia has emerged over the issue. For example, Dr Susan Wicklund has written that her own abortion was a ghastly experience, but insists that helping people by being an abortionist is very rewarding.[95] Dr Bernard Nathanson, the New York gynaecologist who in 1969 helped to form the National Association for the Repeal of Abortion Laws and who himself performed or supervised some 75,000 abortions, came to the conclusion that the foetus is, in fact, a tiny human being, and so worthy of all protection.[96] He also writes of the excessive drinking,

[89] P. Ney, *Deeply Damaged: An Explanation for the Profound Problems Arising from Infant Abortion and Child Abuse* (Canada: Pioneer Publishing Co, 1997), 2.24.

[90] Jo Wainer (ed), *op. cit.,* p. 103.

[91] Jo Wainer (ed), *op. cit.,* p. 125.

[92] M. T. Reist, *op. cit.,* pp. 13, 17, 19, 65, 212-213.

[93] See Mary Meehan, 'Ex-Abortion Workers: Why They Quit' at http://www.meehan-reports.com/quit.html

[94] E.g. Emily Maguire, 'Lack of choice real threat to women's health' in *Sydney Morning Herald,* 4 January, 2006.

[95] S. Wicklund, 'Telling the Stories Behind the Abortions', *New York Times,* 6 November, 2007.

[96] Cf. B. Nathanson and R. Ostling, *Aborting America* (New York: Doubleday, 1979).

the nightmares, the fears and the pressures associated with the medical staff. Indeed, he says, that 'abortion appeared sometimes to have had a more profound effect on the people who were doing them than on those on whom they were being done.'[97]

In recent times there have been some spectacular changes of mind on this issue, including Dr Nathanson who has gone on to denounce the culture of lying associated with the abortion industry which has made a habit of falsely inflating the figures for the number of illegal abortions in past ages and the number of maternal deaths resulting from abortion.[98] In the USA it was routinely claimed that before abortion was legalised, there were about 5,000 to 10,000 deaths per year due to illegal abortions. Since his change of heart on the issue, Nathanson has written: 'I confess that I knew the figures were totally false, and I suppose the others did too if they stopped to think of it.'[99] What mattered was the cause, not the truth. It is also incontestable that the number of maternal deaths fell during the twentieth century in the West not because abortion was legalised but because penicillin was discovered.

The story of Carol Everett is somewhat similar. She was involved in selling 35,000 abortions in the United States, and had one herself, and felt the pain of depression, guilt, and shame—even a sense of being raped—as well as the breakdown of her marriage. Finally, she was converted to Christ, and faced

---

[97] B. Nathanson and R. Ostling, *op.cit.,* p. 141.

[98] Cf. B. Nathanson, *The Abortion Papers* (New York: Frederick Fell Publishers, 1983), pp. 40-41, 97-100. The *New York Times* has continued to foster the culture of lying by announcing the results of a study by the World Health Organization and the abortion rights Guttmacher Institute in New York, which concluded that 'abortion rates are similar in countries where it is legal and those where it is not, suggesting that outlawing the procedure does little to deter women seeking it' (*New York Times,* 12 October, 2007)

[99] B. Nathanson and R. Ostling, *Aborting America*, p.193.

her sin honestly.[100] Norma McCorvey also has swapped sides. She was the Jane Roe in the Roe v. Wade case that led to the United States Supreme Court decision of January 1973 when it struck down all abortion laws in the country, and legalised the practice of killing children right up to birth. Ms McCorvey was supposedly gang raped—but that was untrue—and in fact she never had an abortion. She was used and manipulated by celebrity pro-abortionists, and came to work for the Jane Roe Women's Center in Dallas, Texas. Her experience is the human one that 'It's not an easy thing trying to confuse a conscience that will not stay dead.'[101] In Serbia in 2008, Dr Stojan Adasevic, was reported to have embraced the pro-life cause after 26 years as his country's most renowned abortionist.[102]

In the West, where women are warned of possible long-term medical and psychological consequences of abortion, and where use is made of access to ultrasounds to view the unborn child, abortion rates tend to fall, often quite dramatically.[103] The idea is that 'If wombs had windows, more babies would be carried to term.' In Texas after 2003 it became mandatory to warn mothers of the potential consequences they could suffer from aborting their babies.[104] However, this has not proved to be the case in China and India where ultrasounds have detected females in the womb, leading to more abortions. One Chinese dissident,

[100] Carol Everett, with Jack Shaw, *The Scarlet Lady* (Tennessee: Wolgemuth and Hyatt, 1991; reprinted as *Blood Money* in 1992 by Multnomah Press).

[101] Norma McCorvey, *Won by Love* (Nashville: Thomas Nelson, 1997), p. 58.

[102] http:/veneratiovitae.wordpress.com/2008/11/18/serbian-abortionist-becomes-pro-life-activist/20/01/2009

[103] Even *Time* reported somewhat favourably on the role of crisis pregnancy centres (or pregnancy resource centres) in the USA. These offer free ultrasounds in a pro-life atmosphere (*Time,* 26 February, 2007).

[104] See *A Woman's Right to Know* (Texas Department of Health, 2003). For a government document, this booklet is remarkable for its honesty.

Chi An, tells of rampant female infanticide, living babies being thrown out with the rubbish, and babies about to be born being injected with formaldehyde.[105]

The situations in India and China have proved decidedly embarrassing for those feminists who are still able to blush. Both countries have witnessed female infanticide on a momentous scale, and China has a compulsory one-child policy which has led to the deaths of hundreds of thousands of female infants, whether born or unborn.[106] In many parts of China and India there exists a serious gender disproportion, with the number of males significantly higher than the number of females. Truly, God is not mocked; the penalty for sin is sin. A movement that has supposedly championed women's rights has led to cruel violence against young girls in the form of female infanticide and sex-selection abortion directed at female babies. Janet Hadley protests: 'A society which tolerates female infanticide or abortion of female fetuses holds women in contempt, whatever status women may achieve as mothers of sons.' Yet she fears that banning sex-selection abortions will drive a wedge into other abortion laws.[107] It is, of course, a moral dilemma of the pro-abortionists' own making.

---

[105] See Steve Mosher, *A Mother's Ordeal: The Story of Chi An, One Woman's Fight Against China's One-Child Policy* (United States: Little, Brown and Company, 1994).

[106] In January 2006 an article in the British medical journal the *Lancet* suggested that selective abortion had led to the deaths of up to 10 million baby girls in 20 years, despite the fact that the practice of gender selective abortion has been illegal since 1994; see S. Sheth, 'Missing female births in India', in the *Lancet*, vol. 367, issue 9506, pp. 185-186.

[107] J. Hadley, Abortion: *Between Freedom and Necessity* (London: Virago Press, 1996), p. 100.

5. The Central Issue

When William Wilberforce rose in the House of Commons on 12 May, 1789 to urge the abolition of the slave trade, he appealed directly to Christian principles, although he also admitted that 'I have urged many things that are not my leading motives.' In Wilberforce's words:

> There is a principle above everything that is political; and when I reflect on the command which says 'Thou shalt do no murder', believing the authority to be divine, how can I dare to set up any reasonings of my own against it? And Sir, when we think in terms of eternity, and of the future consequences of all human conduct, what is there in this life that should make any man contradict the dictates of his conscience, the principles of justice, the laws of religion, and of God?[108]

There are very compelling arguments against abortion on the grounds of the welfare of the woman—and it may well be that the battle against abortion in the West may be won incrementally, bit by bit—but the Christian's opposition to abortion must firstly and firmly be based on the Bible's teaching concerning

---

[108] J. Wolffe, *The Expansion of Evangelicalism* (Nottingham: IVP, 2006), pp. 183-184.

the unborn baby as God's image and so protected by the sixth commandment. The infant has a right to life, and the rest of the population has an obligation to protect the life and welfare of the unborn.

The right to life must take precedence over all other rights such as the right to freedom or the right to happiness. This has implications that need to be faced when we come to consider cases such as pregnancy resulting from rape or an unborn child who is deformed. That these are sad cases, worthy of all compassion, must be admitted, but this should not cloud the central issue. Too often, the evangelical case against abortion has backed down on just this point. Michael Hill, for example, is one of many evangelical writers who is unclear where he stands regarding abortion in the aftermath of a rape. [109]

In the case of rape, a number of things might be said. Firstly, a resultant pregnancy is extremely rare. Secondly, if any law allowing abortion in such cases is to mean anything, it would require a conviction first in a court of law—and that, of course, takes months. To waive the need for a conviction first would open the door to abuse of the law. But thirdly, and most importantly, if abortion is wrong because it destroys human life, we must face the fact that the same consideration comes to the fore in the case of rape. Edwin C. Hui reluctantly accepts abortion for rape on the grounds that the mental health of the woman may need to be protected. [110] Yet earlier he had cogently argued against this very position by pointing out that 'An act of rape simply cannot be erased by committing a second unjust act—abortion.' [111] The

[109] M. Hill, *The How and Why of Love* (Kingsford: Matthias Media, 2002), p. 227.

[110] Edwin C. Hui, *At the Beginning of Life: Dilemmas in Theological Bioethics* (Illinois: IVP, 2002), p. 334.

[111] Edwin C. Hui, *op.cit.,* p. 332.

baby should not pay for the sin of the assailant, and the woman's trauma of rape should not be made worse by the trauma of abortion. Hence abortion must be rejected even in this difficult case.

A similar conclusion must also be reached if the unborn child is likely to be severely disabled in any way. To advocate abortion on the grounds that a child may be disabled strikes at the very core of man's view of his fellow man. Peter Singer, who in 1999 was appointed chairman of Princeton University's misnamed Center for Human Values, considers that 'killing a disabled infant is not morally equivalent to killing a person. Very often it is not wrong at all.'[112] Even Dolores Dunnett, who argues that 'prenatal life is sacred and must be protected', writes in her own chilling way:

A friend of mine had to sacrifice a Down's Syndrome child in the hope of having a normal healthy child. The malformed child would not have made the bearing of a healthy child possible because of the medical expenses that would have resulted from the birth of the former. The decision was made to abort the malformed fetus. This proved to be a wise decision, because another fetus was conceived and turned out to be a healthy, beautiful child. The sacrifice was worth it.[113]

As the Western world sought to understand what had happened with the onslaught of Nazism and to rebuild after its associated horrors, Major Leo Alexander saw that a 'slippery slope' had been at work. For decades before the Nazis ever came to power, Germany had flirted with the practice of euthanasia. From 1939 to 1941 Germany officially endorsed a euthanasia

---

[112] Peter Singer, *Practical Ethics* (Cambridge University Press, 1993, reprinted 2006), p. 191.
[113] Dolores E. Dunnett, 'Evangelicals and Abortion' in *Journal of the Evangelical Theological Society*, vol. 33, no. 2, June, 1990, p. 224.

programme directed at all those who were weak and disabled. Some 70,273 are supposed to have perished but the figure is probably higher,[114] with Leo Alexander writing of 275,000 perishing in the killing centres.[115] Alexander's conclusion was also his warning: 'It started with the acceptance of the attitude, basic in the euthanasia movement, that there is such a thing as a life not worthy to be lived.'[116]

The Bible declares in opposition to that, that life which labours under some handicap is not worthless. We do well to remember that Beethoven was deaf, Michelangelo and Dostoyevsky were epileptics, and Helen Keller was both blind and deaf. William Wilberforce had cause to express his gratitude that as 'a small, weakly man', he was not born into a society where such infants were exposed.[117] And where does the Singer approach to life and death end? The evangelist and philanthropist George Whitefield, after all, had a squint. Against this outlook must be placed the joy and blessing that have come to people who have had to look after disabled children.[118] Biblically, care for the disabled is seen as part of a believer's reverence for God (*Lev.* 19:14). It is God who made all human beings, whether disabled or not, so an assault on the person with a disability is an assault on God (*Exod.* 4:11; *Prov.* 17:5). In a sermon on Elizabeth's words to the virgin Mary (*Luke* 1:39-44), Calvin saw the need both to honour all human

[114] Victoria Barnett, *For the Soul of the People: Protestant Protest Against Hitler* (New York: Oxford University Press, 1992), p. 118.

[115] Leo Alexander, 'Medical Science under Dictatorship' in *Ethics & Medicine,* vol. 3, no. 2, 1987, p. 27.

[116] Leo Alexander, *op.cit.,* p. 31.

[117] K. Belmonte, *365 Days with Wilberforce* (Leominster: Day One, 2006), reading for 2 September.

[118] E.g., J. Haggai, *My Son Johnny* (Illinois: Tyndale, 1978); Dale Evans Rogers, *Angel Unaware* (New Jersey: Spire Books, 1953, reprinted 1980); John Wessells, *Conversations with the Voiceless: Finding God's Love in Life's Hardest Questions* (Michigan: Zondervan, 2004).

beings and to humble them. He declared that 'Even the greatest of men is like a miserable earthworm, unless God, out of sheer generosity, chooses to thrust him forward.' He then went on to ask: 'For why is it that we often rebuff our fellow men, and are puffed up with pride and arrogance, each of us wanting to come out on top? It is because we are blind to the gifts God has placed in each individual. If we respected them as we should, we would surely find something of value in the biggest simpleton under the sun!'[119] God surely sends deformed children into the world to minister to those who consider themselves well-formed.

The author has vivid memories of a visit he made as a student pastor to a country hospital in Australia. I had to minister to an old woman who seemed to have completely lost her mind. For many months, all she had done was sit in a corner of the hospital and jabber away incoherently. My attempts to speak to her were totally unsuccessful—she continued to stare blankly and jabber away while I tried to speak. I was at a loss as to what to do next, but finally decided that I would read to her from the Scriptures. As I read from John 14, she at once fell silent and nodded as if in agreement. Whenever I stopped reading and tried to converse, she resumed her incoherent jabbering, but whenever I returned to the Scriptures, she fell silent again. I have no idea what she understood, if she understood anything, but perhaps some light from God's Word was getting through to her. If so, God was indicating that he did not think her life worthless.

Abortion has always been opposed by Christian orthodoxy, from the time of the early church through to the present day. Tertullian put the Christian case as succinctly as anyone:

---

[119] John Calvin, *Songs of the Nativity: Selected Sermons on Luke 1 & 2,* translated by Robert White, (Edinburgh: Banner of Truth, 2008), p. 15.

For us murder is once for all forbidden; so even the child in the womb, while yet the mother's blood is being drawn on to form the human being, it is not lawful for us to destroy . . . It makes no difference whether one takes away the life once born or destroys it as it comes to birth. He is a man, who is to be a man; the fruit is always present in the seed.[120]

A similar position can be found stated in the *Didache,* Clement of Alexandria, Basil of Caesarea, Jerome and Augustine. John Chrysostom denounced abortion as 'even worse than murder', as it made 'the chamber of procreation a chamber for murder'.[121] Thomas Aquinas in the Middle Ages indulged in some unnecessary speculation about when the unborn child received his soul, but he was still opposed to abortion.

With the Reformation, scholastic speculation was swept aside, and, as we have seen, Calvin reaffirmed the simpler stance of the early church. It is apposite to cite the views of Martin Luther in this regard. In 1540 Luther was lecturing on the book of Genesis. He reached chapter 25 where Abraham marries again after the death of Sarah. Luther proclaimed that 'the begetting of children is wonderfully pleasing to [God] . . . He is not hostile to children, as we are.' Then he added:

How great, therefore, the wickedness of human nature is! How many girls there are who prevent conception and kill and expel tender fetuses, although procreation is the work of God! Indeed, some spouses who marry and live together in a respectable manner have various ends in mind, but rarely children.[122]

To Luther, it was clear that the God who declares that we are to

---

[120] Tertullian, *Apology,* IX.

[121] Cited in M. Gorman, *Abortion and the Early Church* (Illinois: IVP, 1982), p. 72.

[122] Martin Luther, *Luther's Works: Lectures on Genesis 21-25,* ed. by Jaroslav Pelikan (Saint Louis: Concordia Publishing House, 1964), p. 304.

be fruitful and multiply regards it as a great evil when human beings destroy their offspring.

Two years later, Luther wrote a tender little treatise, entitled *Comfort for Women Who Have Had a Miscarriage*. Here he sought to reassure suffering Christian women that their child did not require baptism in order to be saved. He made it clear that he was not writing for women who resented being pregnant, deliberately neglected their child, or who strangled or destroyed the child.[123] The Christian woman had to bow before the 'strange' providence of God, but could do so in the knowledge that her child who died in the womb had gone to heaven. To Luther, the unborn child was clearly a child.

The Puritan view was no different. Thomas Manton maintained that 'it is murder to stifle an infant in the womb.'[124] The same condemnation of abortion can be found in the writings of Samuel Bolton.[125] In the nineteenth century, the popular evangelist, D. L. Moody, condemned what he called 'fashionable murder', declaring that

> Murder is, of course, heinous of its own accord. But the murder of a mother's own flesh within the womb is a crime against heaven that is the very essence of sin and inimicable with the Christian religion.[126]

A year or two later, in 1869, the American Presbyterian Church met in General Assembly, and thundered out a pro-life message:

[123] Martin Luther, *Luther's Works*, ed. by Helmut T. Lehmann (Philadelphia: Fortress Press, 1968), vol. 43, p. 247.

[124] Thomas Manton, *A Commentary on James* (Edinburgh: Banner of Truth, 1693, reprinted 1983), p. 101.

[125] Samuel Bolton, *The True Bounds of Christian Freedom* (Edinburgh: Banner of Truth, 1645, reprinted 1978), p.132.

[126] Cited in George Grant, *Third Time Around* (Tennessee: Wolgemuth and Hyatt, 1991), p. 99.

This assembly regards the destruction by parents of their own offspring, before birth, with abhorrence, as a crime against God and against nature; and as the frequency of such murders can no longer be concealed, we hereby warn those that are guilty of this crime that, except they repent, they cannot inherit eternal life. We also exhort those that have been called to preach the gospel, and all who love purity and truth, and who would avert the just judgments of Almighty God from the nation, that they be no longer silent, or tolerant of these things, but that they endeavor by all proper means to stay the floods of impurity and cruelty.[127]

Indeed, it is only in relatively recent times that there been any wavering on this issue in the professing Church.

One of the most disturbing features of the whole modern practice of abortion, and its justification, has been the widespread acceptance of the fact that the foetus is indeed life, but that it need not be protected. Linda Bird Francke, a woman who aborted one of her children, admits that 'there was no doubt that life was right there, in my womb.'[128] Yet she still supports liberal abortion laws, and writes of the expectant mother, 'Who is to say what she should or should not do?'[129] Leslie Cannold plays a similar tune:

Any attempt to place a wedge somewhere in this gradual process and declare that before the wedge the fetus doesn't matter, while after the wedge it does, is a decision that is as much a part of the sea of subjective values around abortion as any other.[130]

Despite this concession to reality, Cannold's vehement defence of the woman's right to abort her child remains unchanged.

[127] Ibid.
[128] Linda Bird Francke, *The Ambivalence of Abortion* (Victoria: Penguin, 1979), p. 254.
[129] Ibid. p. 257.
[130] L. Cannold, *The Abortion Myth* (St Leonards: Allen and Unwin, 1998), p. 37.

She objects to abortion on the grounds of sex selection—which usually means the death of the female child—but accepts most abortions as responsible decisions to 'kill from care'.[131] Janet Hadley too has become hesitant about the language of rights, and wants abortion to become more humanitarian.[132] One can pretend nobility when one kills with kindness.

A *Newsweek* article in 1982 pointed out that many who support abortion nevertheless concede that human life begins at fertilization. The article goes on to say that 'the problem is not determining when "actual human life" begins, but when the value of that life begins to outweigh other considerations, such as the health, or even the happiness, of the mother.'[133] Most startling—and disturbing—of all is the view of Peter Singer who accepts infanticide but is ready to acknowledge that 'the opponents of abortion are right to say that abortion ends a human life' and that 'birth is in some ways an arbitrary place to draw the line at which killing the developing human life ceases to be permissible, and instead becomes murder.'[134]

The full implications of this attitude need to be examined; it means that an unborn child is a human being, but a parent still has the right to murder him or her. There is no reason why husbands, wives, grandparents, minority races, or any other troublesome groups should not, at some time or other, find themselves in the same category as unborn children. Abortion has distorted man's view of man.

The acceptance of abortion has a logical connection with the acceptance of infanticide. The fact that human life begins

[131] L. Cannold, *op.cit.,* p. 128.

[132] J. Hadley, *Abortion: Between Freedom and Necessity* (London: Virago Press, 1996), pp. 82-3.

[133] *Newsweek,* 11 January, 1982, p. 42.

[134] Peter Singer, 'Abortion, the dividing lines' in *Herald Sun,* 25 August 2007.

at conception has led some protagonists in the debate to raise the issue of personhood. According to this view, life may begin at conception, but personhood does not, and it is personhood which confers the right to life. Back in 1960 Joseph Fletcher asserted that 'a fetus is not a moral or personal being since it lacks freedom, self-determination, rationality, the ability to choose either means or ends, and knowledge of its circumstances'.[135] This kind of approach led to Michael Tooley's developing the view that 'An organism possesses a serious right to life only if it possesses the concept of a self as a continuing subject of experiences and other mental states, and believes that it is itself such a continuing entity'.[136] Hence some animals may possess more of a right to life than some infants.[137] Tooley's rather arbitrary suggestion is that infanticide should be allowed up to the end of the first week of the infant's life.[138]

Mary Ann Warren considers that the foetus is not transformed into a person at the moment of birth but does become a biologically separate human being.[139] Hence she has no deep objections to infanticide, although she adds that it may not be appropriate in our society.[140] However, it is Helga Kuhse and Peter Singer who have really pushed the issue of personhood. To Joseph Fletcher's list of 'indicators of personhood', they add rationality, the use of language, and autonomy.[141] A foetus and even an infant lack

[135] J. Fletcher, *Morals and Medicine* (Boston: Beacon Press, 1960), pp. 150-1.

[136] M. Tooley, 'Abortion and Infanticide' in *Philosophy and Public Affairs,* vol 2, no. 1, 1972, p. 44.

[137] M. Tooley, *op.cit.,* p. 65.

[138] M. Tooley, *op.cit.,* p. 64.

[139] Mary Ann Warren, 'The Moral Significance of Birth' in *Bioethics News,* vol. 7, no. 2, 1988, p. 44.

[140] Mary Ann Warren, *op.cit.,* p. 44.

[141] Helga Kuhse and Peter Singer, *Should the Baby Live?* (Oxford: Oxford University Press, 1985), p. 131.

these characteristics. Therefore, 'infanticide is compatible with a stable, well-organized human society.'[142] It ought to be allowed until the infant is 28 days old.[143] Indeed, since self-awareness is part of the definition of personhood they assert that 'Infanticide threatens none of us, for once we are aware of it, we are not infants.'[144] Hardness of heart tends to lead to verbal quibbling, and whatever is possible becomes morally defensible.

Only a consistent Christian position can really confront the modern view of abortion; it is not enough to establish that the foetus is a child; one must also establish that human life is precious. Calvin began his *Institutes* with the statement that 'Nearly all the wisdom we possess, that is to say, true and sound wisdom, consists of two parts: the knowledge of God and of ourselves.'[145] To examine the second part, we must ask with the psalmist, 'What is man, that you are mindful of him? And the son of man, that you care for him?' (cf. *Psa.* 8:1, 4; 144:3). Twice the psalmist asks this question. In Psalm 8, the answer comes that man has great dignity—he is created a little lower than the angels and is crowned with glory and majesty (*Psa.* 8:5). In Psalm 144, however, the answer is designed to humble man: 'Man is like a mere breath; his days are like a passing shadow' (*Psa.* 144:4). The dignity of man derives from his being created in the image of God (*Gen.* 1:26; 9:6; *James* 3:9); the misery of man derives from his being a rebel against his God (*Gen.* 3:14-19). There is a deep unity in all of humanity: 'God has made from one all nations of men to dwell on the face of the whole earth' (*Acts* 17:26). Man is thus man, not because of what he does, but because of who

[142] Helga Kuhse and Peter Singer, *op.cit.,* p. 108.
[143] Helga Kuhse and Peter Singer, *op.cit.,* pp. 195-6.
[144] Helga Kuhse and Peter Singer, *op.cit.,* p. 138.
[145] Calvin, *Institutes,* I, 1, i.

he is. To define man in terms of language, utility, personality or knowledge is to miss the biblical point that the preciousness of human life comes from the fact that man is created in God's image (*Gen.* 9:6).

Humanism denies this view of man, and so falls into insoluble dilemmas. Christianity gives man dignity, yet it humbles him; humanism exalts man, yet it debases him. Humanism necessarily leads to inhumanity. Dostoyevsky foresaw just this situation in his novel *The Devils* where the free-thinking Kirilov comes to the conclusion, 'If there is no god, then I am a god.'[146] Soon after this realization, Kirilov commits suicide. It is the dilemma of humanism—man is both god and earthworm; he is the measure of all things, yet he is finite in worth. The result can only be disastrous. As Pascal put it: 'Man is neither angel nor beast, and it is unfortunately the case that anyone trying to act the angel acts the beast'[147]

It was thought that abortion on demand would solve, or at least alleviate, the problems of illegitimacy, suicide, juvenile delinquency, and child beating, but these problems have all increased since liberal abortion laws were passed.[148] The problem is modern man's view of life; he hungers and thirsts after happiness, not realizing that happiness is only achieved through righteousness (*Matt.* 5: 6). In the somewhat clumsy but nevertheless apt words of Paul Ramsey:

> the notion that an individual human life is absolutely unique, inviolable, irreplaceable, noninterchangeable, not substitutable,

---

[146] F. Dostoyevsky, *The Devils* (Victoria: Penguin, 1975), p. 612.

[147] Pascal, *op. cit.,* p. 242.

[148] See Philip Ney for his evidence that the acceptance of abortion has led to an increase in the rate of child abuse ('Relationship Between Abortion and Child Abuse' in *Canadian Journal of Psychiatry,* vol. 24, no. 7, 1979, pp. 610-20). So much for 'Every child a wanted child'!

and not meldable with other lives is a notion that exists in our civilization because it is Christian; and that idea is so fundamental in the edifice of Western law and morals that it cannot be removed without bringing the whole house down.[149]

We are, in Ramsey's view, descending into 'technological barbarism'.[150]

Perhaps there are some who are reading these pages who have been guilty of abortion, who think of tiny waving arms, and who wonder how old the child would be now. For the sin of blood, there is the atonement in blood. To those who repent, 'the blood of Jesus Christ his Son cleanses us from all sin' (*1 John* 1:7). God's grace in Christ was enough to save Moses, David, and Paul—all men who were stained with the crime of blood. Charles Wesley knew of this grace, and wrote so beautifully of Christ's sacrifice,

> His blood can make the foulest clean,
> His blood availed for me.

In 2 Chronicles 33:6 we read of King Manasseh's sacrifice of his sons to Molech, but the story does not end there. Manasseh was afflicted and we go on to read:

When he was in distress, he entreated the Lord his God and humbled himself greatly before the God of his fathers. When he prayed to him, he was moved by his entreaty and heard his supplication, and brought him again to Jerusalem to his kingdom. Then Manasseh knew that the Lord was God.

---

[149] P. Ramsey, *Ethics at the Edges of Life* (New Haven: Yale University Press, 1978), p. xiv.

[150] P. Ramsey, *op.cit.,* p. 46.

OTHER BANNER BOOKLETS

The Priority of Preaching *John Cheeseman*
The Psalter—The Only Hymnal? *Iain H. Murray*
Read Any Good Books? *Sinclair B. Ferguson*
Reading the Bible *Geoffrey Thomas*
Reading the Bible and Praying in Public *Stuart Olyott*
Simplicity in Preaching *J. C. Ryle*
Study Guide for *The Mortification of Sin*, *Rob Edwards*
Study Guide for *The Promise of the Future*, *Cornelis Venema*
The Unresolved Controversy *Iain H. Murray*
Victory: The Work of the Spirit *Pieter Potgieter*
What Is the Reformed Faith? *J. R. de Witt*
What's Wrong with Preaching Today? *A. N. Martin*
Whom Shall I Marry? *Andrew Swanson*
Worship *J. C. Ryle*

For more information about all Banner publications
please visit our website

www.banneroftruth.co.uk